Maui The Writer Presents
The Cheat Code

Dedicated to the those who ended up playing in a game they never asked to be in, when all they wanted to do was love.

FOREWARD

I sometimes wish I could be a fly on the wall. The fly that witnessed Michael Jackson create Thriller . I dream seeing Heath Ledger prepare for The Dark Knight movie. We only see the finished product. I am more intrigued by the process to get to greatness. I have been the fly on the wall during Maui creating this masterpiece. She can write in the middle of a highway. She has the gift to quiet the war and focus. God sends his angels to give us our messages but she controls her own pen? It's amazing a women so young can captivate the masses. Maui's wisdom is far beyond her years. Often I sit back and wonder how does she have so many relatable life experiences that translate to different walks of life? In a short period of time she has given people hope, answers, and strength. Talent is defined as natural aptitude or skill. Being gifted is having natural ability. Hard work is one who is industrious and diligent in carrying out tasks or duties a flat out striver. Some of us will be blessed to acquire one of these characteristics. It's very rare that someone has all three attributes. Maui benefits from hard work, being gifted, and talented. You can't teach a cook to add these three ingredients to a bland soup. I find so many Instagram people not being what they illustrate online in person. Previously meeting her I had my lips to the side. I met Maui in December and instantly amazed and proven wrong, she is the real deal. How can a person be successful, humble, and giving? Another three qualities to add to her personality. When you are an entrepreneur you have to get what you can get, while people still want what you offer. She wont force what she offers down your throat. It's not that she doesn't have to but her integrity won't allow her. Let me explain. There will be people who sell things just to make money. They will lie, promote things they don't believe in, and can be bought. If she speaks of it she believes in it. Keep inspiring. Keep experiencing. Keep listening. Keep writing. Most importantly keep helping. You are truly everything the world needs. Keep letting your mind and heart carry that pen.

Your Brother,
Chad Black

Introduction

Old fashioned in a sense to millennials possibly, I have always been the type of girl who would prefer a good book over video games or electronics. Practically unavoidable now, since we use technology for everything. I could never really understand the people who could stare at a TV for hours playing video games. Is it the rush of something new every moment they play a new game or reach a new level? Or do they enjoy the progress they make each time, when they beat their last high score? Or is it the ability of being a completely different person in this game? The fiction novels I would read made me feel like I was one of the characters in the books. Less confusing and complex than learning how to play video games, books provided me with peace. Besides, who wants to learn how to play a game? Just to keep losing, over and over, hoping you finally win and when you actually do, you are looking for the next game to play since the challenge is over. Ironically enough, that actually sounds similar to what it is like to date and be in relationships in this society. Everyone is playing this game, hoping to get it right, putting all their effort in, only to lose interest when they finally get the trophy or the high score they have been dying to brag about. Then I guess there are some people who finally beat and win one of the best games they have ever played, killing their desire to chase the rush you get from playing; these are the people who end up married. The single people are the ones who just play online with a bunch of people they barely know and the cheaters add strangers to their game that was better when it was just two players. A three player game just doesn't sound right to me. Then there would be the people like me, who prefer books but somehow ended up playing a game they didn't ask to play, but was in the presence of someone who just passed them a controller.

There are some who end up in games, they did not know they were even in to begin with.

In a generation where many view love as a game instead of something sacred, may you be the one who finds the cheat code.

Instructions: When beginning the game you will be able to choose a second player to play this game with you. During the game be mindful to keep your guard up at all times, to avoid anyone getting close to you. Allowing player two to become too close may result in, falling in love, heartbreak, denial, losing yourself or even worse being stuck inside of the game, which will be hard for you to escape from. Keeping your guard up will allow you to protect yourself from any unexpected disappointments. Level one is dating and should be done with strategy. DO NOT, I REPEAT DO NOT enter level one and immediately get attached to any players, give yourself time to see all of their strengths and weaknesses. The player you choose will be who you continue on with throughout the game, one wrong move and the team can come to an end. Then the game must be started all over from level one. The idea of the game is to see how far you can make it or even make it to the end of the game despite the many obstacles that will be thrown at both players throughout different levels. The higher the level, the harder the obstacles will become and it will be up to you and player 2 to constantly make the best decisions for the team and not the individual. I wish you the best of luck and may the games begin.

START GAME

[Insert Username]

LEVEL ONE

Player 1: LoverGirlMaui19

 I remember back in grade school, if we had a crush on someone, finding out if they liked us back was as simple as a note that said, "Do you like me circle, yes or no?" One circle and you were the one person, someone was eager to arrive at lunch to sit next to or recess for them to see. Boys who were mean to you were only that way because they liked you, or so I thought. If I needed a pencil or if I didn't, the boy who I secretly day dreamed about would be the one I would ask for that pencil from. If you were anything like the adventure seeking children in my neighborhood than you played catch a girl, kiss a girl and would defend her from anyone being mean to your sweetheart.

 The games we played as children we then gathered every last one of them and packed them into a suitcase to take with us where ever we go. I took mine into high school and would never text a guy back fast because he would think I liked him a lot, no double texting, no good morning texting first and if we ever made it to being intimate it was not about chemistry but strategic planning of making him wait. I played chess. The game of strategy, planning, thinking of myself as the queen that is the most powerful piece on the board. Although the pawns could symbolically represent my friends, they were playing completely different games than I was. The more I thought about the situations of the people that I knew, the more I realized although the games were different, it still did not change the fact that we were players. Some better players than others, a few who were getting played, a couple who didn't know they were even in a game and the hopeful ones who found a way to no longer be a part of the game.

Recently I had the chance to ask my friends about the bad relationships that they have been in, what they have learned, what red flags they ignored and even what they could have done differently. Along with my own experiences I decided to take all of the stories I was told and compare them to different types of board games. Using the lessons that we learn as cheat codes to help us the next time we find ourselves in the middle of the game of love. Maybe if there was a cheat code we would have a better chance at winning or avoiding being a part of games we do not want to be in. Unfortunately, some experiences have taught many of us, either we play or we will be played.

Deserve

You deserve to feel everything love has to offer
I may not have much to offer
But what I do have
I will give you half
You do the math
You deserve sunshine
You deserve to laugh
Someone who will ask questions bout your past
Just so they can love you more
A person who gives to you genuinely
Because with partnerships
There is no keeping score
I love you more
You hang up first
I fuck up
You don't bash me
You help me learn
You help me grow
But what do I know
You'll keep getting half ass love
Until you put you first
Lowering your levels of love
For people who won't rise to meet you
I can't even fault you
That has been me too
I want peace for you
You take care of everyone
When is the last time you had someone
Pour into you
Losing yourself in places you don't belong
When is the last time someone loved you for you
So busy pointing out all of your flaws
They can't notice those exact things
Make you beautiful too
I wish you long days
With no stress
Good sex

Someone who will offer their food to you
Who accepts you for who you are
But sees more in you
And their love calms your soul so much
That you can finally see it too

Finds You

I pray that love finds you
You become open to trusting again
After being lied to
Find peace with the memories you get to keep
But the people you must leave behind you
Stop trying to create a husband
Out of someone you too busy
Being a mom to
I want that for you
I want you to bloom
You are a gift to this world
The things you endure
Still hopeful
Still trying
Even after being disappointed some more
I hope you don't stop praying
After receiving what God was preparing you for
I wish you levels of peace so high
Things that used to break you apart
You no longer react to
But more importantly
I hope whomever you love
Finds themselves
Before they find you

Giddy

I want you to find the type of love
That makes you nervous and giddy
That leaves you dreaming
Staring at you while you eating
Just wondering what you are thinking
Talking about their dreams and no matter how far fetched
You know they mean it
You believe it
They can look at you a certain way without saying a word
You know exactly what they are thinking
Do not sell yourself short
It is okay if your soul has been craving more
You have to be specific
So you can receive exactly what you
Have been praying for

The Cheat Code
Game: Jenga
Players: Multiplayer

Jenga was my game of choice. I was in a relationship where I had to be careful about everything I did or deal with everything I thought we built falling apart. Of course it would be my job to put the pieces back together, because it was always my fault, that is just how things were. In the middle of the game I realized that love is not feeling like you are walking on eggshells, in love it may be my responsibility to protect your heart but, it is no fucking responsibility of mine to protect your ego. The responsibility is not mine to bite my tongue, to not voice how I feel because your lack of ability to communicate thinks my emotions are signals of an argument. I do not want to be where I must be careful, I want to be where I feel free.

LEVEL TWO: FREEDOM LOVE

Have you ever watched someone sit and play a video game for hours? Or even a game of chess? Tuning the whole world out and focusing only on, what is right in front of them? They become lost in the game even more if they are passionate. Well, that is what I wanted someone to give me. I wanted love to consume me, to be the reason that the rest of the world seemed silent. I wanted to get lost too. Being so deep in love that nothing else in the world seems to matter or is worth being distracted by. Distraction may cause you to lose what is right in front of you. In high school I wanted to drown in someones love.

My definition of love was defined by quality time, that was my love language then. Your feelings for me could only be shown by spending all of your time with me. That also included random texting throughout the day, talking on the phone until we were practically falling asleep on each other, going out together all the time and including myself in anything they enjoyed doing. Too much of a good thing is never good. People enjoy feeling wanted, but who actually wants to feel consumed? Unless they want to fill their own personal voids with the presence of another person. I was using these relationships to fill something that I felt was missing.

When I could not get the satisfaction that I was looking for, they became another game in the closet that I outgrown or saw no use for. With young love we are players in the game unintentionally, we barely know who we are to even have the slightest clue of what we want, developed. We are kind of just figuring shit out, entering a game with no instructions. As we grow older many of us still find it hard to enjoy the experience of just being with a person and enjoying our time, instead of consuming them. I asked my best friend, "If there was any relationships you had where you wanted to spend all of your time around the person, what do you think was your reason for doing so?" She responded, "Because I did not trust them". But my guy friend said, "My ex made me so happy that it wasn't anyone else I wanted to be around, not even my own friends". At any point of your relationships have those been your reasons too? Spending all of your time with a person because you did not trust their actions behind your back? Or because you have found a place that feels better than any other place your heart has dwelled? A place that feels so good, that there is not any other place on this earth you would rather spend the majority of your time.

My favorite cheat code is freedom. Giving your partner the freedom of being their own individual, valuing their personal space, allowing them to be themselves, because with freedom you will see what a person would rather do with their time. We have a way of coming into peoples lives, disregarding any responsibilities that they may have had and assuming that they should be able to make as much time as we need them to for us, because that is what we would be willing to do for them. I cannot even remember how many times, I have been willing to switch my entire life around, for a relationship or all for the sake of love. Just for me to walk away having to find myself all over again. We change our routines, we spend less time with our friends, some of us slowly start replacing the things we used to love to do, that made us who we are, with whatever we can include our partner in.

Is this what they meant by sacrificing and compromising in relationships? Giving up the things that made that person fall in love with you in the beginning? I want you to experience the most deepest of loves while keeping in mind that a portion of love is freedom. Love that gives you the desire to be courageous, to be more, to live, to do the unthinkable in a good way, but never to pull you away from who you are, unless it is because of growth. The more love that you have for a person the more you should want them to experience your love without the feeling of being confined.

Cheat Code:

You have to be able to love a person so much that your heart
alone, brings them freedom.

Wildflowers

I am attracted to you more
If you are committed to growth
Beautiful, wild, so free
Similar to jungles
Where wildflowers grow
I'm not perfect
But I do my best
Formally known as the girl
Who would always give until she had nothing left
These days I'm selfish
I'm growing
I'm learning
To not lose sight of the bigger picture
Or attach myself to things that don't align with my purpose
It is fuck you
Or I love you
It is balance
It is falling down ten times
But still getting up and trying
It is texting your friends great advice
While you're in the bed crying
It is seeing God in everything around you
But still praying today they don't try me
It is calmness
No Ego
It is finding love inside of myself
Instead of looking to receive it from other people
It is lonely
But it's worth it
Who said it would be easy to break generational curses
It is still loving
It is forgiving when they ain't even sorry
It is creating boundaries for yourself
Still not feeling sorry
Its wild and free like jungles
Where wild flowers grow
It is forgiving people
For what they do not know

Overthinking

I want to love you
Without overthinking
Fighting these
Mental battles about if it's too soon
If my career is more important
And there isn't really no room
Are you keeping it real about how you feel
And your intentions
Or are there ex's you're still connected with
You consciously forgot to mention
I know you love the fact I listen
Ambitious but can be submissive
With all the sexual things I want to do to you
I can't do anything if we don't build a friendship
Who are you loyal to
What's important to you
Can you communicate properly
Or is your pride worth more to you
I don't want to overthink things
But I find that so difficult
This is how I prepare myself
For the plot twists
Or being hurt by you
I want to lay on your chest and sleep in
Vacay with our phones off
Travel the world with my best friend
I don't want to overthink
It steals the peace of enjoying things
Or maybe the moment isn't perfect
The way I feel like it should be
I can't even enjoy the vibe genuinely
Without questioning what you want from me
I just want to feel something
That for once does not need questioning
It will just happen naturally
If its meant for me

Given Up On Love

I hope that you haven't given up on love by the time that I meet you
Or your time isn't occupied by a million different people
If so would you make space for me
Too embarrassed to even look you in the eyes because all I see is a king
I'd spell our names out with kisses on your chest
I came to gift you with things that bring you to your highest pinnacles
Without sex
Because they are priceless
Too easily impressed by bad bitches
I fear you may not know what a wife is
Were your parents married?
Do you want kids?
Are your spiritual?
You look out for all your homies you ever get tired too?
I know as a man you don't always want to express
The things going on inside of you
But if you ever need a friend
I have some time and some ears
I could lend to you
If you ever need support I'll cheer for you
Even after all the work is done
I'll still be Michelle for you
Or if you want to run the world together
I'll be Bey for you
Have this whole world fall in love with things
I wrote for you
While you watch me perform
Knowing that even the things I wrote
Before even knowing you
Are meant for you
I spoke you into existence
Before I even knew a soul like yours even existed
Just don't change
Or end up apologizing for something you lied about
And you hate you got caught
So you flip it on me
Just to make me feel it's my fault

Certain things I can't compromise with
Even for you
I can't give you my love if it interferes with me loving me too
If you not ready it's cool
But you know what they say
One persons I'm not ready
Is someone else's
The moment I saw her knew

Cheat Code:

What is meant to be yours will never require force.If you find yourself forcing something, just know, you may not be the key for that door.

Peace

I wanna be your peace
And as easy as that may sound and seem
I go through shit just like you
Take the world off her back and carry it
She will create heaven on earth for you
The most beautiful man I have ever met
Despite your flaws
You're so open and honest
So as far as my knowledge
I have seen it all
I think you're beautiful still
It's way more attractive when you can keep it real
Let me pray for you
Cook you something
Lighten up the day for you
Rub your feet while we're in bed
Before I have my way with you
The strongest woman in the world
Will cater to a man who does
Exactly what he's supposed to do
When's the last time you've been in love
You ask me the same and I really don't recall
Because it ain't never feel this good
So honestly I don't think I have ever been in love at all
Let me be your peace
Running late for work
Up all night talking about our dreams
We didn't even get no sleep
As much as I love an expensive date
When it comes to you
It never matters what we do
As long as you are here with me
I heard you have been looking for your peace
Similar to the feelings I be getting
When you are here with me

I will give you a piece of me
For a piece of you in return

LEVEL THREE: YOU BELONG TO YOU

Realizing how meaningful having our own freedom is, makes us question how much freedom does our love provide? Do we give others freedom, to continue to be their own individual when they are in a relationship with us? Do we become possessive? Do we now look at it as a partnership, where we compliment each other as team players and are both assets in each others lives? Or is this your better half? What does your love bring? What does your love feel like?

The intentions of my love have been genuine and pure. When I love you, I mean well. I also have learned, that my love has not always felt like freedom, but instead, places of confinement. When you have gone so long watching the things that you love, slip through your finger tips, you grow this sense of never wanting to lose anything that you feel like is yours. I have watched my love leave me and go love someone else. I have watched my love go love someone else, in ways that it has promised to love me forever.

Most of us never want to experience the pain of having to transition from a season with a person who in reality was not meant to be with you forever. So we play this game of strategy, focusing so much on how to avoid this from happening again. Projecting our fears that we have developed from past relationships on fresh starts and what was meant to be clean slates. We may bring trust issues with us during this level. Where are you going? What are you doing? Why did you not answer? Not purposely our intention to be overbearing or excessive but, the fear we have makes us want to catch something before it starts. Before you know it, we are similar to over protective parents in relationships where we were supposed to bring freedom. Doing everything in our power to stop our child from making any mistakes.

Ironically enough, there were times were I have been more focused on being someones mom than their partner or lover. Trying to raise, build and control them into conforming into who I wanted them to be for me. A person who loves you would not try to change you to make you better fitting for them, they would want you to be a better you, for yourself.

So how do you love? Or how do you allow people to love you? When we are honest, open and accountable we can grow. Now when I attempt to build any type of relationship or friendship I make sure I allow people to continue to be who they are. I do not want to be the reason that you can no longer be you or do certain things all because of what I will say or think. Allow people to be themselves so you can see who they truly are. Once you see them, either accept it or let it be. Some will rise to meet you on your level others wont. One thing I know is that love has no room for possession or control.

You belong to you, I belong to me, but it feels good to get a chance to experience each other.

Cheat Code:
Have the ability to reciprocate the things that you ask for,
meet the standards of your own expectations.

Vacation

You have been my vacation
To escape this madness
Clean slate
Trying not to compare
To past shit
Beach house
Four kids just relaxing
House wife
But at night
You know I'm your bad bitch
I mean queen
You know what I mean
I like my man low key
And all about me
Throw me the keys
On the road to your destiny
Let me awaken your dreams
Let down your guard
Open your heart
Build something too strong
To be tore apart
That's the goal right
I'll get to meet you twice
If all of this goes right
Once here
Then again in paradise
Your sunflower
Your best friend
Your fairytale ending
On why it never worked out with any of them
It's true
Pointless to reach my highest pinnacles
If I can't share it with you
I do not want to do this with anyone but you
I adore you more cuz you lift me up
Don't you ever forget about us
Better yet don't forget about me
Your shooting star
All you gotta do is look up
Your good luck charm

No Savior

Seems like everyone around me is in love
Although I've never been the girl into rushing
Yesterday while in bed, I put a Rolls Royce on my goals list
In the spot where I used to have a husband
Thinking of new things to accomplish that mean nothing
When you celebrate them alone
Is there a such thing as being too independent
A little to strong
Too much of I don't need a man
Fuck these guys
Just to find out I was wrong
Still not in need but I have wants
It's easier to receive if you are honest and blunt
I had dreams of a big family
Grateful enough that I have a son that's been enough
Kinda awkward when people write you off like so i guess you
Just one and done
Are you going to have another baby
Maybe....
Focus girl
I don't need favors
I don't need no Superman
I don't need no savior
I need quiet dinners alone at tables
Across from a good man that I can compliment and make greater
So in love with my dreams I forgot to wake up
Or allowed life to rush my timing and find a short cut
Or convince me that since I'm not looking for another half then I can't possibly be
whole enough
Especially not on my own
Waiting on my season, enjoying the happiness I created on my own
When you let things happen naturally
In comes what you've been waiting for all along
Seems like everyone around me is in love
Grateful enough that these days loving myself has been enough
So when my season comes
I have some extra love overflowing to pour into my mans cup

Aligns

Everything eventually aligns
Exactly in the order that it should
Turn back the hands of time
Switch somethings around
I wouldn't do it if I could
All that hurt made you hopeful
And I love the way you shine
Despite the things that you go through
In a world where
We've been looking for miracles and sunshine
Conversations that ended too soon
Trying to accomplish every goal on your bucket list
Find time for yourself
I will always make room for you
Room to listen
To be your voice of reason whenever you find yourself tripping
Or your ego booster when you've been humble way too long
And I tell you babe go get em
Go out there and pop your big shit
I feel like we all need this
People who love puzzles
In a place where we ended up in a million tiny pieces
A reality that sometimes needs escaping
So on the last stop on a midnight train to Georgia
You see me out there waiting
With a sign that's saying
You have a heart I don't want to play with
I got a warm bed for you to lay in
Your friend for you to pray with
Keys to inner peace that feels amazing
And in your eyes it all finally makes sense
All of that shit
Was so things could align
Exactly like this

The Cheat Code

There are many games and tricks that I have played on myself. Some of the games I have played ended up benefiting me, while others ended up hurting me beyond anything I could imagine. My most favorite ones, were the ones that taught me something at the end. This level is similar to, the lies that we tell ourselves. The first lie I told myself at the beginning of many places I had no business being was, "Maybe that's not really a red flag," and "everyone deserves a chance". The reality is, everyone deserves a chance at life, but not a chance with you. You are the catch, you are the prize and if they also view themselves the same, then they will carry themselves a certain way. I made excuses in the moments I needed to be accepting. If you want to believe it or not, somewhere down the line, a person showed you exactly who they were and you did not want to believe them. You ignored signs, you tried to change them or you tried to give them everything that you actually wanted them to give and do for you. I wonder if a piece of us finds some type of thrill, knowing a person is a certain way and believing we can be the one to change them. Maybe we can bring out something in them that nobody has ever been able to do before. A very valuable cheat code I have discovered when dealing with people who refuse to change is realizing, that it just ain't my fucking job to force them.

Cheat Code:

Stop falling in love with potential, in places there was no
potential to begin with.

LEVEL FOUR: BLURRED VISION

This level involves a game that we all have played before, the only difference between this game and the others are, this is one of the few games, that we actually play by ourselves. It is more of a mind game actually, us not believing or accepting people for who they are. We will love, care and see so much potential in a person and the first time they show us their true intentions, we will make excuses for it or simply ignore it.

What is so interesting about this to me is that, most of the people that I know end up leaving a person for the exact things they ignored in the beginning? What keeps you in these places where the pictures that you have painted for a person are not reality? I have personally stayed because, this is the person that I wanted it to be, if that makes sense.

This is the person who I was attracted to, who I loved, who I have already day dreamed standing next to on our wedding day. My sister says, "We stay because we are too lazy to go start over with someone else". There was a big part of me that was comfortable with certain people. But why? After several times of crying, being lied to, let down or shut out. How does a person still feel like they do not deserve anything more, than being somewhere that no longer emotionally satisfies them?

Every person that I have been with who has proven to me that they did not belong on the pedestal I had them on, has gained more confidence in showing me their true colors, once they realized I would still make excuses for them. If we are being honest, I am not even sure if it was the nurturer in me that just wanted to stick it out with someone and feel like I was the reason they changed or began to view life differently. I was drawn to people that had so much inner work to do, people who could not be accountable even if I accepted them for who they were.

These type of people allowed me to also continue to make excuses for myself and the things about me that I just was not ready to acknowledge. In my mind, any flaws that I had weren't as bad compared to the people I was with. Even when I did try to just be patient and hope they would change or at least go back to anything close to the person they were when I met them, those changes would never last very long. Let us be realistic, if there are moments of happiness, how long does it last? A couple weeks? A few days? A person cannot change until they are ready to, even if they love you with everything in their soul. You cannot force anyone to do anything, that they do not want to personally do. Even if they tried to change for you, it would be hard for those changes to last long if they do not also want to change for themselves.

Yet and still we find ourselves trying to get people to change back into who we thought they were or what ever layer of themselves they introduced us to, when we first met them. If there is anything that I want you to learn from this book, I pray it is the value of patience. With time people always reveal exactly who they are, but if we rush too fast into things we will be falling in love with a persons first layer.

Let us make a promise that the next time around, not only will we be patient in getting to know a person, but we will pay attention to their habits, their personality and their values. Truly giving ourselves a chance to understand them better and accepting them for who they are or what ever level they are on in life at the moment. Also knowing that I can accept you for who you are and also not fuck with you for that exact same reason. It is not your job to lower your frequency to meet them nor is it your job to wait around for anyone to change. The best thing that we can do is inspire someone to do more by working on ourselves. Who knows what your taste in people will be like after you have grown even more as a person.

Skipped Class

I skipped class when they gave out lessons on love
Important information like
Until I do this for me
The things a man brings
Could never possibly be enough
Or even if I made him wait
With no intentions
He will still leave right after he fucks
But a man who sees his future in my eyes
Will lay me down and make love
Knowing the value of balance
He'll grip me up and be rough
Some men build homes
Placing their children in it
Who give up long nights at the bar
Casual sex with women
For forehead kisses during Sunday dinner
2am in my panties and bra
Sitting on the counter of our kitchen
Telling you about my day
As you look at me
As if I am what your soul
Has been missing
You don't even say a word
You just listen
They gave out lessons and I missed them
Allowing my heart
To be a pathway of healing to the men who visit
Who never knew love
From being emotionally unavailable or distant
With abandonment issues
Or they daddy was missing
They gave out these lessons and I missed them
Allowing my heart
To become a pathway of healing to the men who visit
Overstaying my welcome
Building solid foundations

Out of places I was only supposed to visit
They gave out lessons and I missed it

Gravity

I have been known to fall in places
That have no landing
No gravity
No longer in control of what is happening
I feel hopeless
Right next to a person
Who puts in just enough effort to make me feel hopeful
Make me feel special
So we create these fairytales in our minds of falling
Praying that they will be the one to catch us
Which does not really take much
Especially coming from a place where there was no love
Praising people for the bare minimum
That will watch you free fall
If you love me hold my hand
Close your eyes
While the only thing thats on your mind
Is I don't give a fuck where we land
As long as it is you that I am next to
Not focused on whose gone catch who
But out of all the people to fall with
A hundred times over again I would choose you
If I am the one than prove it
It is so easy to say you will do anything for a person
That does not require you to do shit
If I am the only person always on your mind don't lose it
Don't lose your train of thought
Then after a fight you are ready to give up
Or you forgot why you fell in love
Do not tell me to jump if you are not ready
Making me believe you would be the one to catch me
Do not say a word if you don't mean it
Because I might love you so much
That I will believe it

Cheat Code:

Even with art you have to step back to get a clearer view of
what you are looking at, its the same with people.

Outgrow

We have been standing in the rain
For what seems like forever
It aint no need to trip
What we gain after a lost
Has always been known to be way better
Calling they phone after a text
Like don't act like you don't see my message
It just sucks doing things alone
After making plans of doing it together
But you know how it goes
Either it's forever
Or we outgrow
Even if time was moving slow
I'd fast forward it to the ending
Just to see where this goes
No regrets
Just love
A couple wish you wells
And some fake love that felt so real
I blamed myself for not being able to tell
It's cool
So pure of heart
That even after devil moves
I chose to see the angel in you
Gave you the type of loyalty
That the shit you hated
You know I hated too
Cross me you don't get a chance to do it again
Look at the bed I made for you
Be so loyal that you betray yourself
I'm only human
Part of the reason I still got love for you
Or the times you really needed me
It was so hard for me to say no to you
It's really actually comical
You can't turn to the people you give your energy to
I loved you with no conditions
Tell this world I never wanted shit from you
The ones who love you
But ask for nothing, are who you are supposed to give everything to

The Cheat Code
Game: Connect Four
Players: Multiplayer

All of us are good at basic math correct? Simple mathematics like 1+1=2 and
2+2=4. I was the master champion of connect four in many of my
relationships, catching them in a lie, remembering something that did not add
up to what they were saying now or calling them out on their bullshit. I was the
world professional champion, of putting two and two together to connect four.
The only issue was, after I connected four I would release all of the pieces and
we would start the game over again. I played this game until I couldn't
anymore, connecting four and doing absolutely nothing. What was the point of
knowing exactly what a person was doing to go against the commitment we
have with each other, just for me to cry for a few hours and then forget how
they made me feel, as if nothing ever happened? I remember in the beginning
when the game was different, we would put two and two together to find
different ways to love each other, to make the relationship better, to grow, to
build a friendship. All of that fades away the moment that you decide to drop
all of the pieces and pretend nothing ever happened. Every time you return to
entertain that game, the odds are against you, your values, your principles and
the pressure the other player feels to change goes away. Change for what? For
who? For the one who will connect four and still play? For the one who does
not want to see anyone else, come along and play a game they have been
playing for so long? So they stick around because of the time they have
invested.

LEVEL FIVE: FORGIVE YOU, FORGIVE YOU NOT

Many people of different ages and genders, ask me frequently, how did I go about forgiving people? Forgiving my partners in past relationships? Forgiving myself for decisions I have made or forgiving people who have hurt me? One of the best cheat codes if you ever find yourself on the forgiveness level of your life, is realizing that there is no rush and that the forgiveness is for you. It takes too much energy to hold onto pain, you are doing yourself a disservice when you hold on to things that would help you grow if you let go of them.

In love I have rushed and forced myself to forgive my partner. Regardless of what it was for. Not to say there were never times that I was the one who sought for someones else forgiveness. I have made mistakes also, that I have needed forgiveness from. I have rushed to forgive in love because, I felt as if, if I did not forgive them fast enough they would leave me or show no effort in trying to gain back my trust. Majority of the time I was not ready to forgive, which is why the more trust that was lost, the more time I felt the need to spend with them. A huge part of me felt they would go behind my back and do the same thing again. While this other part of me blamed myself and wondered what could I have done better. I thought if I would have been a better partner than they would not have had any reason to hurt me. I always found a way to partially blame myself. When in reality they did exactly what they wanted to do. This forgiveness needed to be for me.

Be honest about what you see when you look at them, sometimes they have not changed at all, but we are just tired of being mad at them and we miss them.

So we accept them back in as they are and end up disappointed when they end up putting us through the exact same things that they have done before.

Times where I have done absolutely nothing wrong, I have apologized first because I knew I would be waiting for an apology forever from the person I missed so much. I was the girl who would text first, call first, initiate having a conversation about what happened or telling a guy I don't want to be with them and cover the door as they try to actually leave. I have never allowed anyone to show me they would fight for me, show me they were remorseful for hurting me or show me compassion.

I created this cold wall of not wanting to forgive anyone, because I was tired. I felt like my life had been spent in the middle of a game of "sorry", the only issue just was, I was the one who was always saying it. That wall of not wanting to forgive anyone got higher and higher. Eventually I was just like the people who in my eyes had no compassion. I was carrying around the weight of everyone who hurt me, that I would never forgive and soon I just became exhausted. You get tired of exhausting so much energy into remembering to not forgive these people, so much energy in replaying scenarios back in your head to remind you exactly why you won't forgive them in the first place. You have to reach that level where you want to free yourself from holding onto anything that is not yours to carry around.

The unwillingness to forgive and the trust issues that it develops, travels unto the next relationships we try to build. Our mind convinces us that we have to be ready for history to repeat itself. It makes us believe that what and who has hurt us will happen again, so it is our job to make sure that it does not happen.

Refusing to fully let anyone in or give a fair chance to a person we once loved that may have changed.

Even with learning to let go of the burdens I have carried with me from my childhood, has helped me in my process of forgiving people. We carry so much on our shoulders, for so long. I had to forgive the people that I promised I would hate forever for the things that they have done to me. People who had taken advantage of me in the most horrific ways, I had to forgive, for me.

Telling myself, that the situations I experienced growing up, were not my fault. If I could forgive people who were not sorry, I could also forgive myself and even the people that I have once loved.

Understanding that with my forgiveness, did not come a superficial, fake relationship. It did not come with me pretending that nothing ever happened and looking at the other people completely the same. After all, they still showed me who they were and I have to believe them, even if I forgive them. I can also absolutely forgive and still have no desire to be a friend or have a relationship with that person. But if a person has shown true effort in showing they are apologetic and I decide to forgive them, it is fair to say I must do just that, forgive. Not just say, "I forgive you", but bring up what they have done any chance that I get.

Go into forgiveness with an open heart and remember that this is for you, when you are ready.

The Cheat Code
Game: Sorry
Players: Multiple

Same mistakes just a different day. This game is for the person who is always sorry. No matter what it is that they do to you, you always find yourself right back after one text or phone call. "I am sorry" or "I miss you" seems to always does the trick. This never ending cycle that we grow used to from people, who do not believe that we will ever leave them. So they provide us with the bare minimum of apologies or a few weeks of appearing to have their shit together for us. Then before you know it, they are back to being exactly who they truly are which is one sorry ass person.

Cheat Code:

The things that you don't want to forgive yourself for,
deserve your forgiveness the most.

From me to you

I feel like your soul has a toxic hold on me
No matter how hard I try to escape
I cannot break free
Running in place trying to grab the beautiful memories
From the beginning
Dangling right in front of me
But I can never catch them
So lonely sitting in silence
Practicing for the hundredth time
Exactly what I will say
When I tell you I'm done with this
I'm tired of trying
It's clear you won't change
You touch me and then
We start our toxic cycle all over again
You know my body better than I do
In the moments of me giving you
The most intimate parts of me
I feel loved
I feel adored
Right after you cum
I lay there feeling worse than before
I wish I could understand what your soul is saying
Through your heart beats
Through the way you touch me
You're a man of many talents
The only thing you never mastered was how to love me
I'll be gone by the time that you read this letter
I don't regret meeting you
I only wish that I would have listened
The first time I promised myself
I was leaving you

Sincerely yours,
The girl you never loved

No Words

I am not really good with words
But I do my best when it comes to you
When I weigh the options of my pride and losing you
It's not that hard to choose
I wonder when I'm upset do you think of me
Is next to me the only place you'd rather be
Do you think of losing me
Or does time away make you happy
Do you start showing yo ass
Pulling out all of the sides of you I never see
I'm not perfect
The fact that you aren't either makes
This whole thing work
But eventually you have to grow up
I can't always be the one who speaks up first
The one who initiates
Or who reminds you how I enjoy flowers and romantic dates
Effort is a reflection
At times I question, if I do more than I should
Having to even ask myself that question at all
Makes me feel that the answer is already understood
Do I over love you and give you extra
To compensate what I don't feel is reciprocated
In hopes it will somehow make you better
Do you enjoy me for this moment
Do you sometimes imagine our future together
Whatever
Maybe I just ask you too much stuff
Trying to pull answers out of you
Since you're a man of few words and at times you don't say enough
I'm not really good with words
I know that neither are you
But one thing I have learned over time
Is that when a man really wants you
Even if there is something he doesn't do
He will switch some shit around for you

Heart Of Hearts

If I could do this again I probably would
Even though in my heart of hearts
I know we still wouldn't get it right
Because if the third time is a charm
Then after the second time
I left your ass and took you back
We would have got it right
But it's better to have loved and lost
Than to never have loved at all
Right?
I'm grateful to have had a chance to experience you in this life
What season were you
Leaves are known to fall off in the winter
In the spring time so many things bloom
But you remind me of April
Thunder storms worth of tears you didn't deserve
I wish I could take back the loyalty I gave you
I wish I was a little more patient
Gave you a little more time to bloom
To grow
To get as comfortable as you are when you are alone
And let them true colors show
Was it me
Did I rush with us
When I took my love and planted seeds
Thinking I was pouring into a garden where roses would grow
When the whole time I was growing weeds
Although someone may find beauty in them
They don't do nothing for me
And no matter how many times
I tried to sprinkle rose petals on you
Or paint you red
I could never force you to be
Anything you could never be for me
You only remind me of April

Blinded

I never wanted to love another man
The way I loved you
I was willing to deprive myself of love
To prove
That no matter what you did
Even behind your back I would be loyal to you
A stranger to fair exchanges
I knew I couldn't expect the same from you
Love will leave you blinded
Don't know where we going
But we know it's something better
We just praying that we find it
What was supposed to make you feel alive
Has made you feel so lifeless
Diamonds aren't a girls best friend
Just keep it real thats something priceless
The one I would risk it all for
Is the one who got me crying
I'm supposed to be your queen
Yet you treat me like an object
Saying I have issues
I need to go address my father
What was once your priority
Turned into an option
You give a person all your love too soon
It gets taken for granted
There goes our problem

The Cheat Code
Game: Operation Board Game
Players: Multiple

Meeting you was like walking into a place I have been looking for my whole life without knowing. You were my sanctuary on chaotic days, my therapist when my world was a mess, but my most favorite role you played was my doctor. You healed a heart that was once broken. My body was yours to explore, I loved you. At the points in time I did not know myself, I loved you more than I loved me, naively. I laid on the operation table and watched you take your time with every last part of me. You helped remove my trust issues, put to rest my insecurities, you put faith where fear was, gave me stability and removed my guard. I held you on such high of a pedestal that I could not imagine what life would be like without you, I did not even remember what life was like before you. So good with your hands, so careful, so precise, how could you be so careless when reaching for my heart? My nose did not light up red in this game, but my heart shattered. In the same hands that once held it, at the same place I came to for peace and not too far from the pedestal I held you on. You promised me you would be careful, and in the same breath I could feel how you felt. We were only playing around, it wasn't that serious, nobody was supposed to get hurt.

LEVEL SIX: THE RISK

I cannot think of any game that has the potential of being as risky as falling in love. It takes bravery and courage. As good as it may feel, you are highly aware, that you run the risk of all the other things that happen when you're in love, that nothing can prepare you for. Yet and still you decide to love anyway, which is admirable.

Even after experiencing everything that you have when it comes to intimate relationships, do you truly go into it absolutely being yourself? Or do you come into it with a little hesitation when it comes to completely being who you are? When we gain interest in someone, we begin to think of the right things to say, agree that we have the same interests or the same taste in music. If you are anything like me, in the beginning you appear to be a very nonchalant, mellow soul and then once you are finally comfortable you let every ounce of the emotional person you are show.

But what if we could actually get to know someone and not turn it into a game? A game of, "Well I texted you first yesterday", "I'm going to wait for her to call me back", or "I can't double text because I'm going to seem too needy". What if we all could come into the level with an open mind and willingness to just be exactly who we are? What if the first gift we could give to the person we become interested in, is the gift of transparency? Or a disclaimer, kind of like the way they have on the cover of video games that say, rated R. Except ours would list the things that we are to uncomfortable to initially admit.

If my ex came with a disclaimer it would list things like, romantic, goal oriented, selfish, manipulative, charming and insecure. It would also say, includes, baby momma and several unofficial relationships. Things that a person may not be willing to openly express on their own, we could know before going in and save us so much time. It would allow us a fair chance in deciding if this is a person we would want to continue to pursue or build with. But since that is not how life works, we enter love with just being hopeful.

My disclaimer would list things like, risk taker, blunt, introverted but social, passionate or hopeless romantic. We unintentionally rush things when the chemistry is undeniable and we get a feeling with someone that makes our heart feel like, we have met them before. If we were more patient with getting to truly know people, there would be no need for this disclaimer.

Last time I was in love, it took 4 months for my honeymoon phase with that man to end and for me to see them for who they truly were. But that honeymoon phase, whew. It was ecstasy to me, it was everything that I had never experienced from anyone before and it made me feel high. Their love was the most unhealthiest drug to me. I loved them even more because of how they made me feel, the confidence and the affirmations that they gave me on the daily made me feel unstoppable. They made me feel like the most beautiful, creative, woman in this world. Not realizing how much of my worth I put into their opinions of me, he also had the power to make me feel lower than I had ever felt in my life. The person that I loved so much, convinced me that they loved me more than anyone in my life has ever or more than anyone I would meet after them. Loved me more than my family, my friends or anyone who I viewed in a similar positive light, I had once viewed them. My attachment to them and the control that they had over me made me believe, that what they said was true. I was lost in the game that I played with them. This is what I meant when I said, "You could get lost in the game". As much as being with them hurt me I could not figure out how I would leave them. Whenever I tried to find my strength to leave or focus on me they found a way to manipulate me into believing staying them, just was not that bad.

When a person knows they do not deserve you they become insecure and try so many different ways to bring you to such a low level, you feel like you won't be able to make it without them. Even in the moments where he made me feel like nothing, I still chased the high I had when we first met. It was a cycle of me promising myself I would leave them alone forever and never take them back. Then after a few weeks I was back to giving in, the moment they would text me like nothing happened. I knew what it was like to be addicted to something, that was not good for me. I discovered how powerless this game had the ability to make me feel, if I allowed another individual to control the rules and dynamics of this game for me. Or if I was so unsure of who I was, that I granted another person the honors of defining me. It seemed like the more toxic the relationship became the more passionate the sex was. The sex was the only time that I actually felt any real emotions. I had their attention, I felt passion, I felt wanted and having their body against mine was intoxicating to me. That turned into wanting to have sex all the time so I could feel what I did not get to feel on a daily basis with them. When there was nothing left for me to stay with them for my sexual attachment made sure I would stay a little longer. What I once thought was love turned into a sexual soul tie I could not find my way out of.

Am I ashamed? No, I am not. At that time I loved, with all that I knew. No instructions, just a few things that I have learned from experiences in the past. You learn so much about what love is, when you experience everything that it is not. At that time there was not a person in this world that could convince me that, I was not in love or that this was not my soul mate. But it was not love, I was attached to my ideas of them. After the rain stops, the fog clears and we have a chance to look back and self reflect, I think it is safe to say that many of us have looked back on a level asking ourselves, "What the fuck was I doing?"

Cheat Code:

Everything that love could not be for you, will show you what
you need to be to yourself first.

Switch

I know I said I wasn't doing this love thing again but
I would switch somethings around for you
I see heaven in your eyes when we make love
Do you look down at me and see an angel too
I want to vacation with you
I want to pray with you
Be nasty and eat amazing food
Raise children with you
I waited for you
And I looked up our zodiac signs and we're compatible
But a part of me feels like I'm not ready
Always the person who gives way too much
I have seen the darks sides of love
And I know where that shit can get me
I what it's like to have promises broken
To lose trust
To end up with nothing
After pouring from an empty cup
I know what it's like to rush
And keep forgiving someone who keeps fucking up
I'm not sure of this in between thing that people want
I only know how to give all my love
What a disappointment
To have another human being make you feel
Even with all you give its never enough
I don't want that for us

The Cheat Code
Game: Monopoly
Players: Multiple

Too much time invested to leave, even I have found myself in the monopoly phase of a relationship. Emotionally in a space where all you can do is weigh the options and pay attention to the risks. You may have been in a relationship with more than one type of game or in a relationship just based off of one. What I mean when I say, "Monopoly" is, this is a relationship where there is too much invested to just up and leave. Assets, money, children, businesses, or sometimes, it is just your time that you invested. I see it so often, people becoming unhappy but refusing to walk away from what no longer serves them, because there is too much at stake. Change is petrifying to some, even more so when you have to consider all that you are leaving behind or if you will ever find what you are looking for. But everyone knows, "No risk , no reward".

Cheat Code:

Discovering the lesson in everything you go through is the
reward. Sometimes your biggest blessing is inside of the loss
that you think you took. Be aware and willing to learn from
everything you experience.

LEVEL SEVEN: HOLD ON WE'RE LETTING GO

What cheat code is there for letting go and moving on from things that no longer serve us? When is enough, enough? Even when it comes to the things, that have once brought us great joy. How do we finally get the courage to leave what we have gotten comfortable with or leave all that we have ever known?

I have held onto the memories of love, long after love was no longer being served, where I sat. "I would like another serving of love, please". But I received nothing. Even while sitting at the table that I made, in the house I turned into a home, looking into the eyes of a person I would do anything for, yet and still, nothing.

Once we communicate our needs and wants, what is left for us to do after a person shows no effort to, at least try to improve? We can change our approach on the way we communicate, because after all, it is not what you say, but how you say it. If that does not work do we slowly conform for love? Pieces of us just slowly accepting what we do not want, because we love a person too much to have to let them go. That is what ends up happening, we accept that a person just will not change and we adjust to just working around their traits until we finally decide that we cannot take it anymore.

I have loved, love, more than I have loved the people I have been with. At times I was at such a low place in my life, that I desperately craved any type of companionship. Allowing anyone to just treat me however they saw fit, because if I spoke on how I felt, it would only turn into an argument or an ultimatum. "If you are not happy here, why don't you just leave"? I would hear those words and ask myself the same question. Once you stay after those kind of statements, you are showing that person, that you love them more than the things that they put you through. You love the idea of them more than how they treat you, you love them more than being respected and valued.

With absolutely no desire to change, we are now in a relationship with a person who gradually hurts us more and more, since they know, we do not have the courage yet to walk away. Even if we do mustard up some strength to finally put ourselves first, we receive a, "I am sorry" text, "I didn't mean it" claiming we only need closure one last time and before you know it we are back in the bed, next to a person, but still alone. Feeling emptier than we did before.

What amazes me the most is that, when we finally do let go of the toxic relationship, everything around us begins to start working in our favor. Blessings begin to just come from out of the blue, opportunities we were praying for finds us, we get that promotion that we wanted at work, all after removing ourselves from places we were no longer meant to stay. No longer allowing things to block our blessings. But where does this strength come from? And why do we have to wait until we are finally fed up or a person does something unforgiving to make the decision that we deserve more? Are we afraid? If what we search for when it comes to love actually does exist, are we afraid that it may require us to be something, that we are unsure we are capable of yet? Are we afraid that we will fall short in reciprocating what real love will be expecting of us? Or is this love somewhere on a level that we have not reached and we are to lazy to do the inner work to receive what we desire?

I know that it is hard to walk away from people that you love, especially if at one point in time they loved you just as much as you loved them. Do not let the memories of how magical something was in the beginning, make you look pass, how that person is treating you in this moment. Especially if you are the only one making a conscious effort, to make things work between you two. It is your job to be the reminder to yourself of what you deserve, that is your cheat code. Not forgetting what kind of love you are so willing to give to everyone else, not allowing people to come into your life and not meet you with the same passion.

The more that you work on yourself and create your own happiness, your willingness to entertain people who do not see your true value will dissolve. Imagine you being absolutely sure of who you are, what you bring, then someone comes along, thinking they can make you believe that you are much less. You would not want to hold onto something that does not celebrate you.

Everyone will not love the way you do, which is okay. What is not okay, is to decide to lower what you give, all because someone refused to rise. Let go or get comfortable with what you settled for, if it does not make you happy any longer.

Wrong Time

Right person
Wrong time
The pleasure was mine
Maybe we will meet later on in life
Or somewhere else down the line
I loved you before I met you
My womanly instincts kicked in
On how to cater to a man
The moment I met someone so special
You did some fucked up shit
I did too
I don't regret you
The things you did twice
Were only because I let you
Still happy that I met you
I cried the day I left you
But I didn't know love
And we weren't ready
Shedding tears for our unborn child
That last miscarriage made depression
Hit me heavy
Do I ever cross your mind
Are you happy that you met me
I know it's insane
After all that pain you caused me
I still wonder if you are okay
I still think about you when I'm alone
I used to pray to God you changed
We'd probably be married by now
On vacation with our kids
If I got to have it my way
Maybe one day
Right person
Wrong time
But the pleasure was mine
Maybe we will meet later on in life
Or somewhere else down the line
I loved you before I met you

Stay The Same

Reading our old text messages
Watching videos of us singing in the car
I can't help but smile
Nothing ever stays the same
Moments we wish we could live in forever
People we pray won't ever change
I don't fuck with you
The person you painted yourself out to be
Washed away when it rained
Stop creating expectations for people
That's the only way to avoid the pain
I have heard that before
But I fell for you on purpose
I believed you, because I wanted to
I loved you
I showed you parts of myself
That I've always been too afraid for the world to see
You took all of the things that I told you hurt me
And threw them back at me
You're just like them
What happened to us
To trust
To the effort
To two people who loved being alone
But preferred being alone together
I still think of you
I know it's stupid
You ever think about the friendship you ruined
You could have just left you know
If you truly were not happy

Cheat Code:

The goal is to secure the spiritual and emotional bag first.
Everything else that is meant for you will follow.

Shrink

Last night I realized I'm way too much for you
And not just you but anyone who doesn't know themselves fully
Me being too sure of myself may make you uncomfortable
Pardon me
Excuse me
I'm sorry
Just kidding
You talk so much but I rarely hear you listen
And when you do it's not for comprehension
Just to bring up anything else you forgot to mention
But I know people like you confuse love with attention
So I'm patient and I just wait for you finish
What have I been up to
Me I'm still here trying to figure out what I'm missing
Coming to a realization that these people aren't the problem it's just the people I be picking
I used to do this weird thing
Where I would shrink myself
To make dealing with all of me easier for you
These days if you feel like you have to deal with me
Maybe you're the one who isn't enough
No need for convincing
Just I wish you well and fuck you
No knight and shining armor
No Prince Charming
I paid my dues for these views
At a place where you're so clear on who you are
It becomes funny when someone tries to tell you about you

Many Men

I have met many men
Who all had different intentions
Some who were emotionally distant
Others just craved attention
Some had egos too loud
For their souls to ever listen
Afraid of commitment
But brave enough to not use protection
With their temporary friendships
One was fairly decent
Until he cheated
A charming man
That would give me the world
As long as I kept fucking him in secret
I had this teenage love
Who I would watch sleep
Just to admire him breathing
So broken from staying in places
I had no business being
It was too good to be true
It made sense for me to leave him
I had this older guy
That didn't know what he wanted
Chasing the thrill of being young
It became impossible for me to please him
I have been alone for so long
What if when the right guy comes along
I say fuck men I don't need them
Only because when I say that I love you
You know I mean it
They are not just words
This is so much deeper
I will do anything for the people I love
Even if I have to sacrifice my freedom
Its just the problem with that is
Is the people that I have loved
Were not givers of this world
They were only receivers

The Cheat Code
Game: The Price Is Right

As much as we would enjoy having all of the answers or the cheat codes to everything, there is no time frame we can put on growth. There is absolutely no way we can grow if we are not accountable. Being in low frequency relationships and even being unsure of myself as an individual, I realize how not knowing my worth was the result of many situations I labeled as lessons. It is your job to know your worth and not compromise it for anyone. If you allow a partner to determine how valuable you are, unless they truly know your value, which they cannot if you don't, they will always look for a discount, short you or give you the bare minimum. There were times where I thought I knew my worth but allowed someone to negotiate with me, afraid of being alone, I accepted less than what I knew I was worth. If you do not stand on who you say you are, what you bring or how rare it is to meet someone like you, it is actually comical for you to expect someone else to do the same.

.

Cheat Code:

It is my job before anyone else, to value all of me.

LEVEL EIGHT: ME FIRST

If you have ever played a video game with someone who has finally gotten really far in the game, you know they take the game extremely serious at that point. They do not want to share, let you get a turn and if they do, they are watching you play the whole time, to make sure you do not mess up all the work they had to put in or forget to save the game.

Have you ever been on that level in your life? Where instead of taking a video game extremely serious, you are feeling that way about yourself? A point where you have put so much work into becoming a better version of you, growing and doing the inner work. That you refuse to allow someone to just come along and interfere with all the work you had to put in, to finally get to this point?

It takes so much to finally get to a place in your life, where you can look back on everything that you have been through with the ability to identify the lessons and the cheat codes in what you have grown through. There is so much accountability that is required to reach a higher level of growth. If you cannot be honest with yourself, about the areas that you fell short, there will be no way you can reach the next level of where you want to go.

The cheat codes that we develop are what we have learned during this game. What we learn allows everything to become easier for us the further we progress, because of the self reflecting that we have done and the things that we have learned. How do you reach this point of being so focused on yourself? So focused on your own personal growth with no attachments to anyone else?

To finally reach this selfish level, where you are more in tune with protecting your own peace, knowing your worth, pushing yourself to new limits, there had to be a point where you were just tired of a lot of shit. There had to be a level where you were loving everyone else, giving to everyone, motivating the world, while on the inside you were struggling to hold it all together. Until one day you said no, fuck it, I don't have it or I am not in the mood.

At a place in your life where you have been putting everyone else before yourself, you have decided to finally start choosing you and it feels good. Does it feel empowering to know, that you are the player that is in control of how this game goes for you? More than ever it has now also become your job to make sure, you never allow someone to come along and take all of that away from you.

Not in a sense of, not letting anyone assist you, or come along and compliment the person that you already are on your own. But in the matter of allowing someone to come along and bringing you to a place where you lose yourself. The sense of self and the confidence that we discover when we really begin to love ourselves is something that we should work diligently to make sure we never lose or allow anyone to make us forget who we are, out of the love we have for them.

That is the cheat code for the level of being focused on yourself. Never forgetting who you are or your worth. Not allowing people to come into your life and make you feel undeserving. It is remembering that you are in control.

Doormat

I love you
But
My intuition tells me you are no good for me
Holding on to the person that you used to be
But there is no rewriting history
There is no going back
Remember the times you use to make me
Smile
What happen to that
What happened to us
Now I drown
In tears
Feeling like nothing I do is good enough
And you stare
Don't even flinch
You hate the woman that I have grown into
You liked me better when I was your bitch
When I was your doormat
When I loved you more than I loved myself
I have mastered the art of being alone
Now Im drowning
In happiness that I created myself

The Cheat Code

What has love been willing to do for you? You have given so much to everyone, to lovers, to friends and now I wonder what do you have to show for it besides these lessons, you claim you have learned? You keep wondering why things always end up the same but the truth is, you have not advanced to the next level, because you have not learned the real lesson. You press restart and enter the game trying to win with the same strategies that have been proven to never work. I have been stuck on a level I could not escape from, no matter how hard I tried I could not beat this level. Consistently asking myself, "What the hell am I doing wrong?" Trying to win with the same tricks, the same mindset, the same routines, I realized that in order for me to reach any higher level, I had to become a whole new me. I needed to become a new player. The only issue was I did not want to play. I just had not reached the level where I got to experience the 90's R&B type of love, the level I am on is filled with a generation with signs that read, "Either play or be played". So if for now this is my only option, let the games begin.

LEVEL NINE: DO THE WORK

What I believe many people at times forget about loving themselves and self worth, is that everyday it is your responsibility to make it happen. Everyday you have to decide to make the best decisions for you. Especially when you are new to this level and you are just discovering how difficult it can be some days to not result back to old habits. Some days will be harder than others to not send that text, to not post that quote on social media, to not go back to that relationship or not look at the old pictures that only remind you of what could have been. Every single day, you have to choose things, that choose you. You have to be willing to let go of any shit that does not compliment the journey that you are on or that does not make you want to fall in love with yourself, even more than you have done on your own.

Nobody talks about the accountability that is required or the honesty that it takes. They mention self love like it is this new trend that everyone is trying.

Some nights it becomes so lonely. When you have been craving for something deeper and all you seem to be surrounded by is people who can barely make it pass your surface. You start to realize how easier it was for you to just settle for so long. Now that you have created boundaries and are making healthy decisions you are able to clearly see how some people you would have been quick to text back fast do not even deserve to be around you anymore.

You make the decision of being committed to yourself and being your own best friend in the moments you would look for another person to fill these voids. This is also not becoming so self consumed that you begin to have this I do not need anyone complex, I do not have time for nobody, I do not need any help or I do not want to be in love. Those ideas are fine, if they are because we are working on ourselves, but not when they cause us to no longer be emotionally available to receive or be receptive to love. It also is not to become guarded and not allow anyone in, because you have convinced yourself, that your love is the only love you will ever need. We all crave companionship, friendship, support and love. We just become more aware of how to be selective and not give ourselves away to just anyone.

Sometimes you will have so much love in your heart to give, that you will just want to give it to the first person who accepts it. If that person just so happens to only be a receiver. They will take, as long as you continue to pour into them, then before you know it, your cup that you filled up, is now empty from choosing to pour into a person who had no intention on pouring back into you.

Be selective. I have allowed my idea of love to convince me that I was worthless, that I was not good enough and at my most blinded phases, I allowed it to make me feel, I had to compare myself to the women they cheated on me with. I allowed it to come into my life and have me question everything I thought I knew about who I was.

At places in my life where I had just had enough of being alone, where I was tired of loving and focusing on me. I wanted to just share all of me with someone. Piece by piece I allowed them to take parts of me and it was okay because at least I no longer had to be alone. At least I had someone to respond back to me when I said, "I love you". Even if my intuition was yelling inside of me,

"They don't even mean it". I was willingly to ignore that to get a taste of what love could feel like.

If only I was able to give that same energy to myself at the time. Since the moment you discovered what love was you have unconsciously focused more on, the love that you can give to others, rather than the love you could give to you. Everything that love could never be to me, I have learned to be for myself. Everything that love was not, has taught me what it should be. That is why it is extremely important to pay close attention to how you feel when you are around certain people. How do you feel when you are around the people you love? What sides of yourself do they bring out or even inspire?

It is your job to protect the happiness that you have created or are learning to create for yourself. Make conscious decisions to also not spend majority of your time with anyone who does not make you feel good, just because of the history that you may have with that person.

Sometimes we go from playing this game with a person that we have grown accustomed to playing with and other times we have to discover the beauty of playing alone. The beauty in playing alone is, there is no games, there is no strategy, there is only you, doing the best that you can for yourself.

Cheat Code:

Until you are sure of your own worth, you will continue to
settle for people who do not understand value.

My Husband

I probably was in the presence of my husband
And didn't even notice it
Because he wasn't a charming ass trap dude
Riding around in some foreign whip
He probably referred to me as queen
Instead of looking at me like the baddest bitch
Placing me on pedestals so high
I was afraid I might fall
I've grown accustomed to accepting average shit
Lost and confused saying nice guys really don't exist
Yes they do
At the time ain't shit is what I liked
And these days guys who don't see your value
Just seemed to be my type
I hadn't discovered my value first
I think I met my husband
Somewhere opening doors for me
Staring at me while I put on makeup
Wishing I could see the girl he sees
Thinking I'm the most beautiful when I dress modestly
And most likely I thought he was a cornball honestly
I know I have met my husband
A nice caring man that I thought was tripping
Because I was too busy falling for people
Who made me beg for attention
Attentive if it will end up in me moaning
But when I speak they doesn't listen
I know my husband is somewhere out there
Praying for a girl just like me
But I'll never see the purpose of a good man
If I don't discover the purpose in me
Hopefully my husband will wait for me

Intimacy

Have you ever
experienced intimacy
Without someone touching you
Speaking life into your soul
You can feel their aura surrounding you
I have never been high like this
I am convinced
Things like this are only heaven sent
Was this you God?
I wonder
He remembered
I like picnic dates in the summer
My favorite color
He listens
I was complete before we got here
Yet he's brung me pieces I didn't know were missing
I've always been a healer
Loving on damaged men
Thinking I'll fix him
What a difference
To be in the presence of a grown ass man
Who doesn't let you lift a
Finger
He only says naw babe I'll get it
It makes me want to let you in it
Turn my body into your wonderland
Keep going even after you finish
You make me want to listen
All without force
Telling you I appreciate you
You're so calm as if the pleasure is yours
You didn't even have to touch me
But anytime that you do
Plant your seeds inside of me
As if you want them to bloom
The experience is even better
Because of how I feel about you

I Prayed For You

I mentioned you to God then I prayed for you
God please teach my husband patience
I know I technically don't have one yet
I'm also unsure if he is someone I have loved in the past
Or haven't met
Or if he has been here all along
He might be somewhere out there right now
Thinking soul mates don't exist
With concepts of love that are wrong
I don't need him to be perfect just open
No knight in shining armor
No fancy car
Just a man who values teamwork more than ego
To help with building a home that is ours
I want more children
Teach him the importance of family
Of legacy
Of generational wealth
Make his soul filled with humility
I hope I don't sound silly
Praying for a man who doesn't even know
I'll be his wife one day
Teach me how to love without possession
How to listen and trust him to lead
Without any second guessing
I want to be gentle when expressing how I feel without being defensive
Teach me trust and friendship
I want to feel fire when I kiss him
Is he far ?
How long will it take for him to get here ?
I am not looking or rushing
Just trusting
Timing
So I can meet the standards of my own expectations
Upon his arrival
I prayed for you
I will be just fine if I have to wait for you

The Cheat Code
Game: Guess Who
Players: Two Players

I have played the game of ignoring all characteristics a person has and ending up picking the same type of person I have before in relationships. Not realizing that our type and taste in people have been the reason for unsuccessful attempts at love. These people that we claim were horrible ex's, not compatible with us or simply just lessons learned. They did not knock on our doors coming to find us, we picked them. Even if they chose us first we decided to involve ourselves with them. Something about them felt like home, they felt familiar, they felt like the type of people who we always end up choosing. We have been falling in love not with what we need, but with what feels familiar.

LEVEL TEN: SAME TYPE

One of my favorite words is accountability. How willing you are to be accountable makes me able to see how much you are willing to grow. You have to be honest with yourself about your own habits and choices that you make. Even I had to be honest with myself about the people that I continued to choose and why. I have always dated older guys, telling myself they were mature and had a lot more to offer than younger guys. Although, I would find myself going through the same issues with them that I would with guys my age, clearly that was not the reason. I thought about what qualities attracted me to them in the first place, what kept me there for longer than I should have been or what had got me there in the first place. The older guys I dated made me feel beautiful, I felt protected, provided for and secure. They made me feel like I did not have to worry about anything because it would always be taken care of. I have stayed longer than I should have because I had allowed myself to become dependent on them financially and emotionally at times.

The dependency on my relationships did not just happen with the older guys but some of my other encounters too. I would become dependent on their opinions, support and when I would feel as if they were taking that away from me or not providing me with it on the level I needed them to, I felt like I had nothing. I did not always know how to be those things for myself, so I searched for it in the men that I was with.

During this level I don't think it was a partner that I was looking for, but someone who had the qualities of what a father should be. I had daddy issues and refused to admit it. I wondered if my father was in my life and he had instilled all these values in me as child, would I even feel the need to search for this love in men? Would I seek their validation so much? If my whole life my father told me I was beautiful, that I was good enough, that I was talented, would it have saved me from the times I fell in love with someones words before their actions? I have always looked at men to be these providers and safe places for me. I had never viewed them as being my partner or really thinking about their needs. I chose emotionally unavailable men and I have chosen insecure men, who would hide behind the material things that they could provide to make up for their lack of emotional intimacy. For so long I was okay with that, because as long as that man was taking care of home, then none of that was a problem right? Wrong.

Accountability. When you think of the people that you have chosen, do you ever ask yourself why? Even if they were not always that way, why? I hear people say all the time, how all the people that they meet are the same, but, are they the same or do you continue to choose the same type of people or attract the same type of person? If you finally have realized that you in fact choose the same type of people, think about what similarities they have to identify your patterns. Self-Reflection. Have you chosen these people or have you, at times allowed your loneliness to make decisions for you?

My friend who we are going to call Jessica said this when I asked her the same question, "In my last relationship loneliness chose the person for me, I just ended up attached to the first person who gave me real attention, because I was tired of being by myself". When I met him I was working and going to school. I barely went out, so everyday I had the same routine of going to work, going to school, working out and just going home. You start getting tired of sleeping by yourself especially when you feel like you're a good woman. I felt like I had so much to offer but if that was the case why was I alone? I wanted to love somebody and for them to see how much of a good woman I was. I met Dre at the snack bar on campus, he made small talk and asked for my number. It seemed like after I gave him my number, I start seeing him all the damn time on campus. He became my reason to start coming to school looking cute and changing my hairstyles. But where I fucked up at was, we were texting for weeks and he never asked, when could he take me out? After I told him I lived alone, all he would ask was,"When you going to cook for me? I had not cooked for nobody else in so long. So I start inviting him over, cooking for him and before you knew it he was always at my house, eating, having sex and watching tv. I couldn't get him to do anything, but I never made it a requirement either. I just was so hype to have someone around, I start willingly just wanting to show how much of a good woman I was and he didn't deserve it. He did not do anything at all to even work for what I had. So my cheat code to myself would be to stop giving myself to people who do not deserve me. It is cool to be patient and have requirements. I would tell myself to stop being so damn hype to just have a person around, that I forget that my presence is a blessing, period.

Cheat Code:

There will be no more prematurely committing to people who do
not deserve you.

LEVEL ELEVEN: BEING AWARE

The reason that I mentioned that you should allow love in, is because that's the advice that people have given me. After experiencing a heartbreak or finally breaking free from a level we thought we would never beat. The last thing that we want to do is start all over again. I wonder the type of things that you would do or the experiences you would have when finally being loved the right way. You have already shown what you would be willing to do for the wrong person, imagine if you got it right? If you met someone who loved the way you loved or deeper? When that time comes we have to have the ability to be open and receptive to love, without being guarded or assuming we once again have to bring the games that we are used to playing along with us.

By this time you should be self aware and able to identify your own games when it comes to choosing the same type of people. So be prepared if what you have been praying for, comes in a package that you weren't expecting. Making sure that you are in a space that you can also reciprocate what you are asking for. Meet the standards of your own expectations of others. A lot of the time we expect others to do, what we would be willingly to do for them, but honestly are we always in the mental and emotional space to be able to tend to every need a person may have? Even if we are, we have to remember that we all are human and just because a person may not tend to every expectation, doesn't mean they are not trying to show any effort.

I remember about 2 years ago the person I was seeing at the time would always want me to do their laundry when I got to their place twice out of the week. I did not mind, but there were times where work had me exhausted and I still would do the laundry when I got there. I also would fold the clothes (since I can't cook, this little responsibility made me feel needed). One time during the holiday season at my job, I got to their place and said, "I am not doing the laundry tonight, I am going to do it in the morning". This turned into a whole argument of me slacking in the relationship and if you could see the look on my face at the time, it would have "are you serious"written all over it. At the time the relationship was not bad, but the stress that I was under at work made me feel like I was not in the mental space where I could cater to the needs of another person.

It takes being honest with yourself, because even with me feeling that way in my heart I still kept trying, before I knew it, I never felt like doing no laundry or anything they asked me to do. In their eyes I had completely given up putting forth any effort for the small things that mattered to them, despite how willing they were to do anything that I asked them for. It wasn't because I did not want to, I just felt like I barely had enough energy to give to myself let alone another person. I think back and wonder why did I never just communicate that with them, instead of allowing them to believe it was something they were doing wrong?

The lack of communication game reminds me of playing charades. Just trying to guess or assume how a person may be feeling or what they are thinking. It is one of the most unfair games to a person whose only intention is to have the ability to properly love you. Lack of communication, the fear of being vulnerable and transparent, make it so difficult for a person to be able to give to you what you need at the capacity that you want it. They will always be playing charades and you will not always be satisfied when you are assuming that they should just know what's wrong or what they should be doing. Even if a person comes along and does know how to naturally do things that you enjoy, what if you don't know how to love them in the language that they understand? Would you not want them to communicate with you what you could be working on? One of my most common games as a woman has been telling my man that nothing is wrong with me then when he says, "Okay" and continues on with what he is doing, then I come in with a 5 page essay on where he fucked up at. How can love fully enter a home that has many different lock combinations on the door? Or is this your way of being cautious about what you have seen happen in the past and you just want to take all the proper measures in protecting your heart? Do you think by not communicating it shows you how much they care to figure out what's going on with you? There are no rewards in not communicating, continuously choosing to date the same type of people or assuming people should have these psychic abilities when it comes to what you want.

Cheat Code:

Eventually you will get tired of running away from love, you will finally see how beautiful it is, if you run towards it.

The Cheat Code

My plan was never to be a player in this game we have created involving love. In fact, I have given almost everything my heart was capable of, only for me to still lose in the end. I have changed things about myself, I have compromised, I have been vulnerable, whatever it took so that in the end me and my team player would win together. I have watched that same player leave me to play the game alone while they took everything I taught them, to go play with someone else. I realized sooner than later that, in order for me to no longer be apart of the game, I had to conquer the hardest part of it, the level where my heart and mind were at war. My heart has played some unforgivable tricks on me. Do you understand how difficult it is going through life knowing that your heart has the capability of experiencing a love that would make you betray yourself? Make you go against everything you thought you believed in. As much as I am tired of losing, my soul is even more exhausted at playing in a game it never asked to be in.

LEVEL TWELVE: END THE GAME

The different phases that you have experienced throughout your life have been the different levels of this one big game we are playing. Every time you have not won or have had to start over, you have gained wisdom, lessons, your cheat codes. If you did not gain anything then you will have noticed yourself on the same level experiencing the same situations. We will continue to go through the same cycles until we finally fully understand the lessons we were meant to learn. Since you will be constantly growing and evolving forever, there will always be new levels and knowledge to get from what's around us. So do we ever really beat this game? Do we ever really win? Yes, we do. You have won every time you have conquered the person that you no longer wanted to be. Every time you have let go of something toxic, broke a habit, took a leap of faith, or walked in your purpose, you have won. Even if those may not seem like the biggest victories to you at the moment, if you really think about it, those are truly the ones that deserve to be celebrated the most. Those were the hardest one to go up against, when they have been what we were comfortable with for so long.

I want you to start looking at love as an experience that you get the pleasure of enjoying instead of this strategic way to create an outcome that will never happen if it is not meant for you. No more overthinking our way out of happiness, start enjoying people and the time that you get with them. No more possessing and trying to control our way into the lives of people who would make room for us if they wanted us to join them. No more over extending and loving people with the hopes that they will finally see our worth and decide to give us the love we feel we deserve from them. No more settling with what in our hearts we know could never make us happy, just because it is a little better than being alone. These are the games that I want you to put an end to. The things that we all have done that seem to never work in our favor. The things that bring us temporary fulfillment but never last as long as we thought it would. You owe yourself the favor of deciding that you no longer want to be apart of this game that this generation calls love.

You will decide to no longer be a player and attract people who have no interest in games. But if you continue on playing or entertaining the very people who have treated your love like an amusement show, you will continue to find yourself pressing the restart button. You have the ability to end the game. All you have to do is decide that you no longer want to play and just love. In the middle of your favorite level, may you find your cheat codes, may you put an end to the games.

Maui.

Acknowledgements

First and foremost I want to give all praise to God. For him giving me the mercy, the opportunity and the ability to live in my purpose. To my social media followers who have become my internet family who I FaceTime when I go live on instagram. I write for me and you. You all have given me this comfortable space to be able to be transparent about the things that I have been through and not once feel judged. I was so afraid to give you another book after knowing how much you loved the first two, I cried so much working on this, I wanted it to be perfect and exceed what I have written before. But I decided to just continue the route that I normally have gone which is just being honest and myself. You have loved what I have written because inside of what I have shared, you could see yourself, your own experiences and the light in the middle of some shit that hurt so deeply. So as normal this is for you and I hope that it inspires each one of you to continue to do the inner work of trying to heal and emotionally grow. I appreciate all of you for just listening.

To my son Azai, you will read these books one day and I hope that you always know that my desire to be a good person has always been so that I could be able to raise one. I love you so much, you are my little best friend and thank you for not being mad at me when I would tell you I was going to Wawa, when I really was leaving out of town to do a show. "See you when you get back from doing that poem stuff momma" is your favorite line for me. I will never be able to put in real words what you mean to me, I am blessed to be your mom in this life.

To my sister India, thank you for helping me and if I never get to tell you enough how much I appreciate you, just know that I do. You get on my nerves but when we aren't around each other, I always wish we were so I could have someone to laugh with.

To Chad Black who has been my official unofficial therapist, accountant, content creator, business minder, bad joke telling, always judging my love life, asking a million damn questions brother, thank you. We did that podcast and we just became real friends. You are one of my close friends that I truly value and I know that you will always be honest with me.

For Britt, I love you so much. God knew what he was doing placing us together, we fit so perfectly. If its watching shows together, trying to predict why our lives are so crazy by reading a horoscope, sending funny memes to each other all day or being on our never ending journey of getting our shit together.

To the Weatherbees who are my second family who just can't seem to get rid of me because all I do is pop up at their house unannounced, thank you. Thank you to Nate "DJ HBK", who has been my family before the poetry and my one and only DJ since I had my first event. It is just going to keep getting bigger and better.

To my family thank you. To my aunts Juanita, Clarissa and my brother Antonio who supported me so much and I lost all of you in a 2 year span, I am grateful to have been able to give you flowers while you were here, but there isn't a day that goes by that I don't miss you so much.

To my friend Terrell, thank you for always being there for me, for loving me through my different phases and even through my emotional breakdowns I would have when I first had my son. Which resulted in me cutting all my hair off, wearing dashikis and colorful sneakers. I am glad we got through that. You give me advice when I did not ask for it and often make better decisions for me than myself because you know me so well. I appreciate and love you.

Lastly, to the men that I have loved. Everything that I have learned from each of you has been the recipes for me to create something so beautiful. Thank you for the experiences, the lessons, the memories and in those moments being what I needed. I do not regret any one of you. To my Travis even though we barely speak thank you for being what I thought I wanted at the moment. Thank you more, for showing me I deserved better.

I know I am forgetting a lot of people so, I am sorry if I missed you. Thank you everyone who has come to a show, read the books, bought a shirt or shared my work. I appreciate all of you, talk to you soon.

-Maui

Made in USA - Crawfordsville, IN
34890_9781089332091
04.18.2020 2351